SuperM

KAI

Jopping

Lyrics by
Tay Jasper / Adrian McKinnon /
Min-ji Kim (Jam Factory) /
Yu-Bin Hwang

Composed by
Greg Bonnick / Hayden Chapman
/ Tay Jasper / Adrian McKinnon /
Nasia Jones / Geoffrey McCray /
Zachary Chicoine / Marcus Scott

Arranged by
LDN Noise / Young-Jin Yoo

Directed by Young-Jin Yoo
Background Vocals by Young-Jin Yoo / Tay Jasper / Adrian McKinnon
Recorded & Digital Editing by Young-Jin Yoo @ SM BOOMINGSYSTEM
Engineered for Mix by Young-Jin Yoo @ SM BOOMINGSYSTEM
Mixed by Young-Jin Yoo @ SM BOOMINGSYSTEM

Original Title: Jopping
Original Writers: Greg Bonnick / Hayden Chapman /
Jeremy D Jasper (Tay Jasper) / Adrian McKinnon / Nasia Jones
/ Geoffrey McCray / Zachary Chicoine / Marcus Scott
Original Publishers: EKKO Music Rights (powered by CTGA)
/ AMM 7 / WB Music Corp. / Jeremy Jasper Ascap Pub
Designee / LIVE ABOVE WIN DAILY / BEACON ELECTRIC
Sub-Publishers: EKKO Music Rights (powered by CTGA) /
Warner Chappell Music Korea Inc.

I don't even care 여긴 우릴 태울 stage
Left to the right, we gon' make it,
make it bang, put your hands in the
air, let me see you bounce
To the left, to the right 시작되는 round

Cuz when we jumping and popping,
we jopping

Jopping X3

You know how we get down
(jopping) How we get down
(jopping) How we get down
Cuz when we jumping and popping,
we jopping

Step on the floor (start a riot)
Where the competition man it's looking
one-sided, up like a 7 forty 7 we the
flyest, a lifestyle you should try it
So 시작해, make it last, front to back
Yeah, yeah (give me that X3)
The roof's on fire let it burn to an ash
We gon' keep it jopping, tell the DJ
bring it back

날아봐 like a paraglide 나타나 in a pair
of slides 떠나자 out to paradise 건배해
to a better life, gotta move, watch the
money monsoon make the crowd go
wild in a small room
Let me see you put it all on like a
costume 어디까지 번져갈지 몰라

We love to move it, keep it going, don't
stop it's in your nature 말해 girl what
you want 춤을 춰봐 we go on and on
Champagne life, that's all you want
Don't stop letting it go

Cuz we got that glow

**REPEAT *REPEAT
Cuz when we jumping and popping,
we jopping

You think ya big boi, throwing three
stacks I'mma show you how to ball,
you a mismatch, opinionated but I'm
always spitting straight facts
Throwback, I might throw this on an 8 track
믿어봐 I'm a sight to see
Ex-ci-ting go and drop the beat
We get it jopping the party, it don't
stop 축제는 이제부터 시작이니까

이 곳이 파티인데 바삐 어딜 가
We'll keep it jumping and popping here
all night, jump to the front if you want
it, hands up 손을 위로
Don't stop letting it go, like you don't care

*REPEAT

모두 hear that sound 틀을 벗어난
하나된 신세계를 펼쳐
Play the music loud 살아나
Cuz tonight's gonna set you free

*REPEAT

I don't even care 한껏 달아오른 stage
Left to the right we gon' make it, make
it bang, put your hands in the air, let
me see you bounce
To the left, to the right 시작되는 round
Cuz when we jumping and popping,
we jopping X2

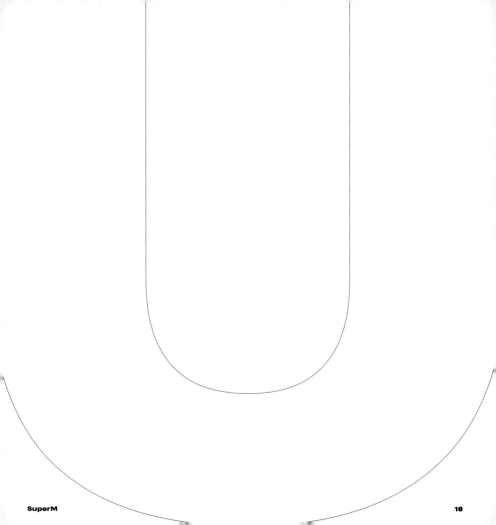

I Can't Stand The Rain

Korean Lyrics by
Kenzie

Composed by
Thomas Troelsen / Sam Martin /
Kenzie

Arranged by
Kenzie

I can't stand the rain, can't stand the rain, rain X4 비가 몸을 타고 흘러내린다
너를 향한 목마름은 더해가 기나긴 이 헤매임의 끝은 넌데 앞을 봐 앞을 봐
감정은 아픔이 되어 번진다 지금 네게 달려갈 수 있을까 차라리 널 몰랐다면 생각하곤 해
Take me back X2

She got me bad, got me going crazy 쉼 없이 너를 갈구하는데
Shouldn't have let you go 비를 멈춰야 했어

I can't stand the rain anymore, I can't stand the cold any longer
너 없이 난 아무것도 할 수 없어 소중했던 것들조차 의미 없어 더운 온기로 채워줘
I can't stand the rain

메말라 소리 없는 외침을 달래본다 심장의 거친 고동에 귀를 대어본다 끝도 없는 헤매임의
끝에 네가 있어주길 원해 비가 아프지 않았던 날들에 아름다웠던 널 다시 불러내
우릴 지켜봤던 jealous eyes, yeah
Take me back X2

She got me bad, got me going crazy 두 손에 흘러내린 빗물에
Shouldn't have let you go 비를 멈춰야 했어

REPEAT

더 뜨겁게 태울래 이겨낼게 널 위해 I won't let it go 찬란한 천국이 되어줘
Ah, yeah I can't stand the rain

She got me bad, got me going crazy
She got me got me bad 쉼 없이 너를 갈구하는데 she got me going crazy

REPEAT

Directed by Kenzie **Background Vocals by** Andrew Choi
Strings Arranged & Conducted by Nile Lee
Strings Performed by ON the string
Recorded by Eui-Seok Jung @ SM Blue Cup Studio /
Ki-Hong Jung (Assistant Dyne Choi) @ Seoul Studio
Digital Editing by Min-Ji No @ SM SSAM Studio
Engineered for Mix by Min-Ji No @ SM SSAM Studio
Mixed by Eui-Seok Jung @ SM Blue Cup Studio

Original Title: I Can't Stand The Rain
Original Writers: Thomas Troelsen / Sam Martin / Kenzie
Original Publishers: Copyright Control (KODA) /
Sam Martin Music Publishing / Artist Publishing Group West
(ASCAP) admin by Kobalt Songs Music Publishing (ASCAP) /
EKKO Music Rights (powered by CTGA)
Sub-Publisher: Music Cube, Inc.

KAI

Korean Lyrics by
danke (lalala_Studio)

Composed by
Greg Bonnick / Hayden Chapman
/ Adrian McKinnon / Ebenezer

Arranged by
LDN Noise

2 Fast

SuperM

한순간에 덮친 기시감 넌 말로 할 수 없는
미묘함 what you say, what you say
now one sec 초침의 한 칸 그 사이에 no,
no, no, no 난 이미 느꼈어 뭔가
한 찰나의 분초 감정의 파도는 높아지네
No 걷잡을 수 없게

네가 딱 한걸음 올 때 내 맘은 저기 별
위를 두 바퀴쯤 돈 것 같아

*숨을 한 번 내쉬기도 전에 나를 사로잡지
2 Fast, 2 Fast, no, 2 Fast
눈과 눈이 스치기도 전에 나를 사로잡지
2 Fast, 2 Fast 아주 작은 세포 하나까지
2 Fast

(keep it moving)
2 Fast (keep it moving)
Oh-ooh (keep it moving)
2 Fast (keep it moving)

Girl, 한계치를 넘은 열기 머리칼이 너로
곤두서는 느낌 뭐라 정의를 내리겠니
내 이론 혹은 명제 따윈 너로 인해
단 한 번에 무너져 나의 세겐 이미 너
이전과 너 이후로 나뉘어 버려

놓치기엔 너무 분명한 내 안에 퍼져버린
강렬함

멍하니 널 바라볼 때 황홀을 헤매다 보니
벌써 밤이 된 것 같아

*REPEAT

짧은 그 사이 모든 것이 너로 가득 차
너로 인해 난 나로 인해 넌 완전해진 것 같아

2 Fast X2
Eh, eh, eh, baby (keep it moving)
2 Fast (keep it moving)
Uh-ooh (keep it moving)
Yeah, yeah, yeah, come on
(keep it moving)

Eh, eh, baby

*REPEAT

(keep it moving) Moving 2 Fast
(keep it moving, moving) X3
(keep it moving) Moving 2 Fast
(keep it moving) 2 Fast

Sung by TAEMIN / BAEKHYUN / MARK / LUCAS
Vocal Directed by DEEZ
Background Vocals by TAEMIN / BAEKHYUN / MARK / LUCAS /
Andrew Choi / Adrian McKinnon / Ebenezer
Recorded by Chul-Soon Kim @ SM Blue Ocean Studio / Ji-Hong Lee
@ SM LVYIN Studio / Sung-Su Min @ doobdoob studio
Digital Editing by Ho-Jin Jung @ sound POOL studios
Engineered for Mix by Ji-Hong Lee @ SM LVYIN Studio
Mixed by Chul-Soon Kim @ SM Blue Ocean Studio

Original Title: 2 Fast
Original Writers: Greg Bonnick / Hayden Chapman / Adrian
McKinnon / Ebenezer Fabiyi
Original Publishers: EKKO Music Rights (powered by CTGA)
/ AMM 7 / WB Music Corp. / Sony/ATV Music Publishing
Allegro (Uk)
Sub-Publishers: EKKO Music Rights (powered by CTGA)
/ Warner Chappell Music Korea Inc. / Sony/ATV Music
Publishing Korea

Super Car

Korean Lyrics by
Seong-Hee Park (Jam Factory)

Composed by
Moonshine / Bobii Lewis /
Charite Viken

Arranged by
Moonshine

Must be the best, I'm
내 온몸으로 시동 거는 drive
떨기 시작한 나의 몸은 꼭 마치 super car
깜빡 켜진 light 내 두 눈이야 뛰는 이 심장
Yeah, 들어봐 내 엔진의 sound
Ooh, we feel it 날럽한 내 소음 sorry
고막 찢는 이 소리 나를 쫓는 너의 눈빛

따라오려 애쓴 허나 태생부터 something
different 흔적마다 blessing
지워지지 않을 매일 위해 running

*움직여 vroom, like a black car
어떤 리듬 다 잘 타 더 vroom 레벨이 달라
나도 나를 감당하기 벅차

**Taking control
You just wanna follow my lead
When I'm in my zone, we just keep
on going and going, don't stop

Drifting, drifting, drifting

뒤쪽 트렁크는 터질 것 같이 너무 많은 내
비장의 cage 자꾸 꺼내도 판도라같이 계속
존재해 날 빛낼 secret
Ooh, we feel it 흥분에 오싹한 느낌
You know that 너의 상식을 침범해 매너
지켜 추월해줄게 화끈한 속도를 보여줄게
넌 그냥 마음껏 놀라면 돼

따라오려 애쓴 허나 태생부터 something
different 흔적마다 blessing
범접하려 하면 이미 난 또 running

*REPEAT **REPEAT

Drifting, drifting, drifting, don't stop X2

나의 몸엔 흠집이 함께해 but 내겐 없어
brakes 끝은 늘 시작과 이어진 way, ooh
Pull up like X2 고삐 풀어 다 핸들을 꺾어
난 우린 pull up like yeah, we pull up like
고삐 풀어 다

Vroom, like a black car 이 리듬에 올라타
더 vroom 겁날 게 뭐야 거침없이 너를
운전해봐

Taking control 질주 끝에 마주한 더 넓은
Brand new zone, we just keep on going
and going, don't stop

Drifting, drifting, drifting, don't stop X2

Sung by TAEMIN / BAEKHYUN / TAEYONG / TEN / MARK
Vocal Directed by DEEZ
Background Vocals by TAEMIN / BAEKHYUN / TAEYONG / TEN / MARK /
Pollen / Bobii Lewis
Recorded by Chul-Soon Kim @ SM Blue Ocean Studio / Ji-Hong Lee
@ SM LVYIN Studio / Sung-Su Min @ doobdoob Studio
Digital Editing by Woo-Young Jang @ doobdoob Studio /
Yoo-Ra Jeong
Engineered for Mix by Min-Kyu Lee @ SM Big Shot Studio
Mixed by Jong-Pil Gu (BeatBurger) @ SM Yellow Tail Studio

Original Title: Driftin'
Original Writers: Jonatan Gusmark / Ludvig Evers /
Bobii Lewis / Charite Viken
Original Publishers: EKKO Music Rights Europe
(powered by CTGA) / EKKO Publishing INC
Sub-Publisher: EKKO Music Rights (powered by CTGA)

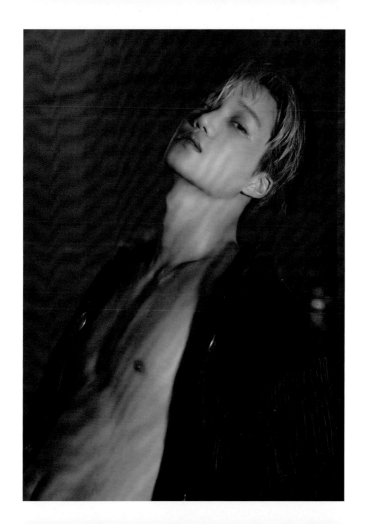

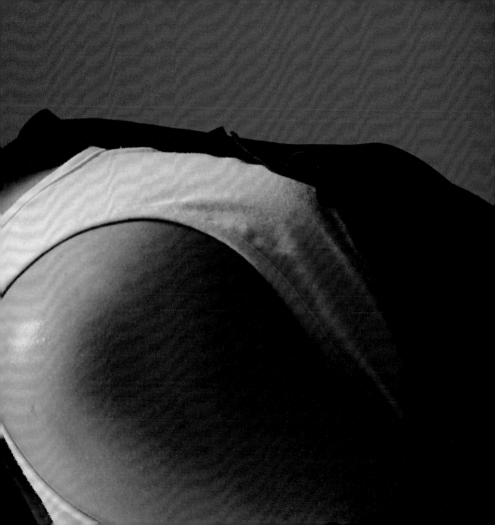

Korean Lyrics by
Yu-Ri Cho / Ran Kim (Jam Factory)
/ TAEYONG

Composed by
Jonathan Santana / Shae Jacobs
/ Tyler Holmes / TAEYONG

Arranged by
Jonathan Santana

No
Manners

*차갑게 말해 with no manners 나쁘게 떠날수록 better
어설픈 배려 따위 됐어 냉정히 끝낼수록 better got no manners

끝인 것 같아 말은 안 해도 삐걱대는 맘에 우린 흔들려 위태로운 한 조각 남겨둔 채로 선뜻
나서지를 못해 둘 중 누구도 꽤 괜찮았던 사이지 이런 감상만이 너와 마주 앉은 뒤 떠오른
한 마디 커피잔에 뺏긴 시선 들은 마치 쉿 죽은 듯이 고요하지 *REPEAT 넌 숨기려 할수록
티가 나 진심을 무심코 뱉곤 했잖아 순간이 모여서 만든 거리감 벌어진 간극을 좁힐 줄 몰라
대단한 일은 아니지 이별 말이야 단지 서로를 갉아먹을 이 맘이 겁이 나지 후유증에 뺏길
앞으로의 날이 쉿 소리 없이 다가왔지 *REPEAT

**한 조각 희망마저 가질 수 없게 전부 버려 한 편의 지나가는 drama
그렇게 생각하면 쉬워 got no manners

Dancing on my backseat, you look so yeah 센치 got me comma, commas,
I'm addicted to you, toxic 내게 달려 나는 달리지 put the pedal to the metal 매달리지
너의 매력 you the answer, never question 우린 없지 got no manners 삐딱하게 너는
낸시 난 시드 우린 beautiful 너무 beautiful, don't say thank you or nothing, criminal so
cynical but we need to learn some manners 빛이 나 빛이 나
I'm addicted to you, toxic X2

*REPEAT **REPEAT

Sung by TAEMIN / KAI / TAEYONG / TEN
Vocal Directed by DEEZ
Background Vocals by TAEMIN / KAI / TEN / Soulman / JANGMOON
Recorded by Ji-Hong Lee, Min-Ji No @ SM LVYIN Studio / Min-Ji No
@ SM SSAM Studio / Eu-Gene Kwon, Sung-Su Min @ doobdoob Studio
/ Seung-Yun On @ sound POOL studios
Digital Editing by Yoo-Ra Jeong
Engineered for Mix by Min-Ji No @ SM SSAM Studio
Mixed by Jin Namkoong @ SM Concert Hall Studio

Original Title: No Manners
Original Writers: Jonathan Santana / Shae Jacobs /
Tyler Holmes
Original Publishers: Morris Street Publishing (BMI) /
Where Da Kasz At (BMI) / Prescription Songs administered by
Kobalt Music Group Ltd / 55 Mega Hurtz (ASCAP)
Sub-Publisher: Music Cube, Inc.

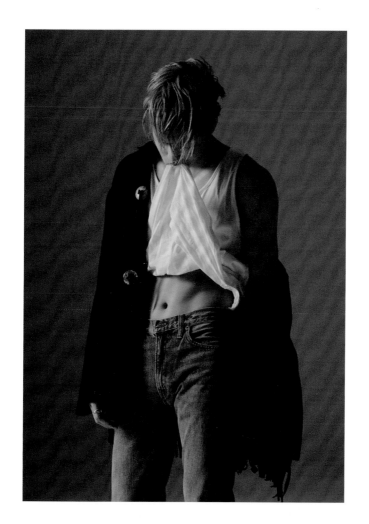

English Lyrics

1. Jopping

'I don't even care here we will burn on this stage Left to the right, we gon' make it, make it bang Put your hands in the air, let me see you bounce To the left, to the right it begins the round

Cuz when we jumping and popping, we jopping

Jopping X3

***'You know how we get down (jopping) How we get down (jopping) How we get down Cuz when we jumping and popping, we jopping**

Step on the floor (start a riot) Where the competition man it's looking one-sided Up like a 7 forty 7 we the flyest, a lifestyle you should try it So start, make it last, front to back yeah, yeah (give me that X3) The roof's on fire let it burn to an ash We gon' keep it jopping, tell the DJ bring it back

Fly, like a paraglide, Appear in a pair of slides Let's go out to paradise, Cheers to a better life Gotta move, watch the money monsoon Make the crowd go wild in a small room Let me see you put it all on like a costume Don't know how far it'll spread

We love to move it, keep it going, don't stop It's in your nature, tell me girl what you want C'mon dance, we go on and on Champagne life, that's all you want Don't stop letting it go cuz we got that glow

***REPEAT *REPEAT**

Cuz when we jumping and popping, we jopping

You think ya big boi, throwing three stacks I'mma show you how to ball, you a mismatch Opinionated but I'm always spitting straight facts Throwback, I might throw this on an 8 track Believe me, I'm a sight to see Ex-ci-ting go and drop the beat We get it jopping the party, it don't stop The festival is now starting

This place is a party but where are you rushing to We'll keep it jumping and popping here all night Jump to the front if you want it, hands up, put your hands up Don't stop letting it go, like you don't care

*REPEAT

Everyone hear that sound Step out of the frame and open an uniformed new world Play the music loud Come alive cuz tonight's gonna set you free

*REPEAT

I don't even care here we will burn on this stage Left to the right we gon' make it, make it bang Put your hands in the air, let me see you bounce To the left, to the right it begins the round
Cuz when we jumping and popping, we jopping X2

2. I Can't Stand The Rain

I can't stand the rain, can't stand the rain, rain X4

The rain rides my body and flows down The thirst for you gets more intense At the end of this long wandering it's you look ahead look ahead Emotions become pain and grow Now can I run to you What if I didn't know you I think about that Take me back X2

She got me bad, got me going crazy With no rest I'm craving you Shouldn't have let you go Should've stopped the rain

'I can't stand the rain anymore I can't stand the cold any longer Without you I can't do anything Even the meaningful things are useless Fill me with warm heat I can't stand the rain

So dry, I comfort my mute cry On my rough hear beat I lay my ears At the end of this endless wandering I want you to be there

On the days the rain didn't hurt The beautiful you I call out Watching us jealous eyes, yeah
Take me back X2

She got me bad, got me going crazy The rain that's flowing on my two hands Shouldn't have let you go Should've stopped the rain

*REPEAT

Hotter I want to burn it up I'll go through it for you I won't let it go become a brilliant paradise I can't stand the rain Ah, yeah I can't stand the rain

She got me bad, got me going crazy She got me got me bad With no rest I'm craving you She got me going crazy

*REPEAT

3. 2 Fast

A déjà vu that strikes in a moment, you are an unexplainably delicate What you say, what you say now one sec, one click on the second hand In between no, no, no, no I already felt something A moment's timing, the waves of emotions rise No it's out of control

When you take one step towards me, it feels like my heart took two laps around that star up high

You captivate me before I breathe once 2 Fast, 2 Fast, no, 2 Fast You captivate me before our eyes even meet 2 Fast, 2 Fast Even the small cells 2 Fast

(keep it moving) 2 Fast (keep it moving) Oh-ooh (keep it moving) 2 Fast (keep it moving)

Girl, the heat is over the limit, I'm getting goosebumps because of you What can we say My theories or propositions collapse at once because of you My worlds are separated into before and after you

Too sure to let go The strong feeling in me spread

When I blankly look at you Since I've been wandering in a trance It feels like it's already night

*REPEAT

Within that short period everything is filled with you Because of you I am and be because of me we're perfect

2 Fast X2 Eh, eh. eh, baby (keep it moving) 2 Fast (keep it moving) Uh-ooh (keep it moving)Yeah, yeah, yeah, come on (keep it moving) Eh, eh, baby

*REPEAT

(keep it moving) Moving 2 Fast
(keep it moving, moving) X3
(keep it moving) Moving 2 Fast
(keep it moving) 2 Fast

4. Super Car

Must be the best, I'm turning the engine on with my whole body drive My body shaking it's like a super car Flash, the lit up headlights are my two eyes, my heart is beating Yeah, listen to the sound of my engine Ooh, we feel it the sound of my fast moves sorry This sound that rips your ear canals your eyesight is chasing me Tried so hard to follow but from birth we're something different Every trace is a blessing, just so I'm not forgotten every day I keep running

*Move vroom, like a black car whatever rhythm I can ride Stronger vroom at a different level I can't even handle myself **Taking control You just wanna follow my lead when I'm in my zone We just keep on going and going don't stop*

Drifting, drifting, drifting

My back trunk is about to explode I have too many secret weapons in my cage Even if I keep taking it out, like the pandoras box it keeps existing it'll make me shine, this secret Ooh, we feel it a creepy feeling in excitement you know that I invade your knowledge keep your manners I'll pass you I'll show you some speed you just need to be surprised

Tried so hard to follow but from birth we're something different Every trace is a blessing if you're trying to catch up to me I'm already running

*REPEAT **REPEAT
Drifting, drifting, drifting, don't stop X2

I'm always with these scars on my body but I don't have brakes The end is always connected to the beginning way, ooh Pull up like X2 everyone undo the bridle I turn the handle We pull up like yeah, we pull up like everyone undo the bridle

Vroom, like a black car hop on this rhythm stronger vroom what is there is fear drive you without hesitation

Taking control At the end of the race, we face a broader brand new zone We just keep on going and going don't stop Drifting, drifting, drifting, don't stop X2

5. No Manners

Say it in a cold tone with no manners the worse you leave it the better No need for awkward considerations the cleaner the end is better Got no manners

I think it's the end even if we don't talk our unstable hearts shake us With one dangling piece left Either one of us make the move first

We had a good relationship, this kind of impression One word comes into mind when I see you sitting in front of me The attention that the coffee cup took Is quiet like it's dead

*REPEAT

The more you tried to hide it showed, you told the truth unintentionally The distance that was made from every moment, don't know how to shorten this gap

Farewells aren't something great it's just I'm scared of this feeling that we'll hurt each other The future that is going to be taken from the after effect Came without a warning

*REPEAT

**Throw away everything so we can't even have a single piece of hope It's easier if you think of this as an episode of a drama Got no manners*

Dancing on my backseat, you look so yeah sentimental Got me comma, commas, I'm addicted to you, toxic Run to me, I am running put the pedal to the metal Got me hanging on your charms you the answer, never question We don't have it, got no manners We are beautiful so beautiful crooked you're Nancy and I'm Sid Don't say thank you or nothing, criminal so cynical But we need to learn some manners you shine, you shine I'm addicted to you, toxic X2

*REPEAT **REPEAT

KAI

Credits

Executive Producer
SM ENTERTAINMENT Co., Ltd.

Producer
SOO-MAN LEE

Music & Sound Supervisor
YOUNG-JIN YOO

Producing Director
Chris Lee

A&R Direction & Coordination
Jung-Hee Chae, Saet-Byeol Jang

International A&R
Kay Kim, Jamie Lee, Emily Oh

International Strategy & Promotion
John Seongjin Yang

Music Licensing
Jung-Eun Oh, Min-Ju Cha, Min-Jung Kim

Music Production Management
Hui-Mok Kang, A-Ruem Yu,
Min-Jeong Park, Sang-Hee Yoo

Artist Planning & Development
Hee-Jun Yoon, Yu-Eun Cho

Recorded by
Young-Jin Yoo @ SM BOOMINGSYSTEM
Chul-Soon Kim @ SM Blue Ocean Studio
Eui-Seok Jung @ SM Blue Cup Studio
Ji-Hong Lee @ SM LVYIN Studio
Min-Ji No @ SM SSAM Studio
Eu-Gene Kwon, Sung-Su Min
@ doobdoob Studio
Seung-Yun On @ sound POOL studios
Ki-Hong Jung (Assistant Dyne Choi)
@ Seoul Studio

Mixed by
Young-Jin Yoo @ SM BOOMINGSYSTEM
Jin Namkoong @ SM Concert Hall Studio
Jong-Pil Gu (BeatBurger)
@ SM Yellow Tail Studio
Chul-Soon Kim @ SM Blue Ocean Studio
Eui-Seok Jung @ SM Blue Cup Studio

Mastered by
Hoon Cheon @ Sonic Korea
Dave Kutch @ The Mastering Palace

Management Director
Young-Jun Tak

Artist Management & Promotion
Jin Choi, Byoung-Jun Kang, Dae-Bin
Kim, Jin-Wook Bang, Tae-Ho Kim,
Eui-Soo Nam, Byung-Yong Choi,
Hye-Jung Han

Public Relations & Publicity
Eun-A Kim, Sang-Hee Jung,
Ji-Sun Lee

Media Planning
Min-Sung Kim, Min-Kwon Bok,
Jae-Heuk Heo, Ho-Sik Kim

Choreography Direction
Young-Jun Tak, Seong-Yong Hong

Choreographer
Keone Madrid, Jawn Ha, Quick Style,
Greg Hwang, Jack Lee, MIHAWK
BACK, ILL(PREPIX), JUST JERK

Contents Marketing
Joohwan Yeom, Jessica Eunjung Rew,
Kyoungduck Park, Jihye Jeong

International Marketing
Mina Jungmin Choi, Keun-Hye Kim

**Customer Relationship
Management**
Eun-A Kim, Yoon-Joo Tark,
Hyo-Sil Yang, Jung-A Lee

[SM USA]

Managing & Marketing Director
Dom Rodriguez, Jeremy Lopez

A&R Direction & Coordination
Janie Yoo, Victor Portillo,
Steven M. Lee

Content Director
Sang-Min Lee

[INDIVIDUAL TEASER]
Video Direction & Arrangement
Min-Seo Jeong
Video Director
Beomjin (VM Project Architecture)

[GROUP TEASER]
Video Direction & Arrangement
Ki-Hyun Kim, A-Reum Oh
Video Director
Rohsangyoon (filmbyteam)

[Music Video]
Video Direction & Arrangement
Ki-Hyun Kim, A-Reum Oh
Music Video Director
Woogie Kim (GDW)

Art Director
Woo-Cheol Jo

Graphic Design
Woo-Cheol Jo, Eun-Hee Kim, Woo-Sik Jo

Photography
Ki-Gon Kwak KAI Ver.
Jang-Hyun Hong United Ver.

M/V Sketch Photography
Hye-Soo Kim

[AR T-shirt Promotion]
Promotion planning & direction
Min-Soo Yoon, Sol Han
Filming
Woo-Jin Jang (MNJ FILM)
2D/3D Motion
Hee-Jin Kim
AR APP
SEERS LAB

Visual Director
Sea-Jun Kim

Visual Planning
Sun-Young Kim, Ye-Rin Kim

Stylist
Wook Kim TAEMIN, BAEKHYUN, KAI
Young-Jin Kim TAEYONG, MARK
Young-Jin Kim, Si-Hyuk Ryu TEN, LUCAS

Hair
Jung-Ho Lim TAEMIN, TEN, LUCAS
Nae-Joo Park BAEKHYUN, KAI
Song-Hee Han TAEYONG, MARK

Make-Up
Jung-Hyun Lim TAEMIN
Yun-Su Hyun BAEKHYUN, KAI
Seong-Eun An TAEYONG, MARK
Eun-Joo Oh TEN, LUCAS

**Management and
Marketing Executive**
YOUNG-MIN KIM, SO-YOUNG NAM

Executive Supervisor
YOUNG-MIN KIM

<Official Homepage>
SuperM Official Homepage
http://superm.smtown.com
SMTOWN Official Homepage
http://www.smtown.com

<Social Network Service>
Facebook https://www.facebook.com/SuperM
Twitter https://www.twitter.com/SuperM
Instagram https://www.instagram.com/SuperM
Weibo https://www.weibo.com/SuperM